Ex
Libris

Lois Lucylle Williams
La Junta Colo May 26-1935

AMERICAN INDIANS

FIRST FAMILIES OF
THE SOUTHWEST

BY J. F. HUCKEL

TRADE MARK

THE THUNDERBIRD

FIFTH EDITION, 1934

PUBLISHED BY FRED HARVEY
INDIAN DEPARTMENT
ALBUQUERQUE, NEW MEXICO

Foreword

Even in the days when Christopher Columbus was a boy playing about the streets and docks of Genoa, there were little republics scattered through a portion of the America he was to discover.

The peoples of this unknown country built many-storied houses of stone, recognized property rights, had their traditions and religions and chose men to make and administer laws. They elected head men and counsellors corresponding generally to our system of mayors and aldermen.

Among some of them, women had rights beyond the hopes of the most enthusiastic suffragette of our time. For the most part they had a regard for law and observed a broad code of morals perhaps surpassing that of the peasants of the days of Ferdinand and Isabella.

The white man first came in contact with these people in 1539 and even then, it is said, their pottery and other handicraft inspired admiration among the Spaniards. These people grew their own cotton, wove it into cloth, dyed it and made it into garments. They had fields and irrigation works—not makeshift individual schemes, but reservoirs and aqueducts that served the entire community and operated on a communal plan.

They traded among themselves, had their own religions and their priests. When it came to war, the Pueblo, the dominant people, were found to be as able as in peace, but they went to battle only in defense.

While their neighbors, the Navaho, were not the equal of the Pueblo in these steps toward civilization, they were far in advance of the Plains Indians of the country north. The first mention of the Navaho by the Spanish explorers is in 1598. At that time the Indians had begun their work in silver, an art brought to them by the Mexicans. Weaving was learned from their Pueblo neighbors. Then when the whites introduced sheep and goats, the Navaho began the weaving of wool and the creation of those wonderful blankets that bear their name, an art in which they have been without equal to this day.

Such were the people of mountain and desert in the new world. Their country was what we now call New Mexico and Arizona, and today they retain the customs of four centuries ago to a degree equalled by no other people excepting the Bedouins of the Far East.

Not all of these early Americans of the Southwest were models of industry, citizenship and domestic duty. The Apaches in those days were as adept in the gentle art of murder as in the 80's, when Crook and Miles finally rounded up their last little marauding band under Geronimo.

It's of these Americans who antedate America that this book tells—of their every-day life, their strange worship, of the men and women and children.

Indians Who Work and Have Never Asked for Aid

"The Pueblo are picturesque anywhere and always; they are Indians who are neither poor nor naked; Indians who feed themselves and ask no aid of Washington; Indians who were farmers and irrigators before the new world was discovered."

In other days, the Pueblo peoples of New Mexico— about whom this was written—were warriors too, but only when war was brought to them.

The Cochiti tribe of the Pueblo live on the Rio Grande, a few miles northeast of Domingo, New Mexico. Once they were a people strong enough to be an important factor in the Indian revolt against Spain, back in the seventeenth century. Now there are hardly 300 of them left on their reservation of 24,000 acres.

When the Spaniards came north from Mexico on their exploration tours they brought with them sheep and goats. The Pueblo obtained sheep from the Spaniards and from that time became shepherds as well as farmers. They wove blankets before the Navaho knew how and were extensive agriculturists, their small fields being irrigated from living streams or from storage reservoirs.

A COCHITI CHIEF

Laguna, a Typical Pueblo Indian Village

Long before the English Colonists had formed anything like organized government on the Atlantic Coast, the Pueblo Indians were living in towns under an elective administration. Each community chose officers corresponding to governor, lieutenant governor and a board of advisers.

Laguna, a typical village, sixty-six miles west of Albuquerque, is one of the later settlements, dating from 1699.

The pueblos, or villages, are generally built in terrace fashion, the upper tiers of the houses setting back from those next below, so that the roofs of the lower houses formed a sort of front yard for those above. With the Spaniards came modern improvements, such as doors and shutters.

In the early days the rooms were necessarily small. The transportation of beams was exceedingly difficult, for horses and beasts of burden were unknown to the Pueblos until the Spaniards brought them. Sandstone and lava blocks were the materials used in construction of the houses. Often the villages were rectangular with open courts, but there was usually little fixed plan of outline.

The Indians learned of the wheel from the Spaniards and built their own vehicles. The wheels of the caretta were usually made from sections of a tree trunk and the whole was constructed of wood, not even nails being used.

For centuries the people of Laguna have been experts in the art of making pottery.

OLD CARETTA
LAGUNA, NEW MEXICO

How the Indian Women Do the Cooking

Before the advent of the Spaniards the Indians generally did their cooking in an excavation in the ground, heated with stones and then filled with food and covered over. For winter supplies food was prepared by drying and preserving.

The Pueblo tribes carried this art of pit cooking further than any other Indians. When the Spaniards came, they taught the Indians to build dome shaped ovens of boughs and twigs plastered with adobe clay and these are in common use today. In all cases these ovens are out of doors, thus keeping the interior of the home cool and livable. Some of them are twelve to fifteen feet in diameter, serving a number of families.

Contrary to general belief, the Indians have always preferred cooked food. In addition to meats, they had vegetables in the form of maize, cactus, yucca, mesquite and agave. The Spaniards introduced European fruits and vegetables and every Pueblo village now has its gardens close by. Maize was prepared by them in innumerable forms. *Pinole*, ground parched corn, is still a favorite dish. They made hominy by removing the coating of the corn with a lye of wood ashes and then boiling.

The Hopi Indians make the strange *piki*, or, "paper bread." A large flat stone, the upper side ebony black and highly polished, is heated to a blistering degree. The mother rubs the surface with a paste of pounded water-melon seeds, which evidently serves the purpose of shortening. Then deftly, with lightning-like rapidity, she applies a thin bluish batter from a bowl. It is baked in a moment and she transfers the wafer-like sheet of bread to a rush mat at her side on the floor. Soon a great pile of the *piki* is stacked up and the sheets are made into long rolls and laid away for future use.

ACOMA INDIANS BAKING BREAD
NEW MEXICO

Indian Women Who Command the Household

No other Indian women, and few of the gentler sex among the white peoples, possess the rights of the Pueblo women. All of the Pueblo tribes trace their descent through the maternal branch of the family and the home belongs entirely to the mother. She may dismiss her husband on the slightest pretext. In that event his only recourse is to leave the house at once, returning to the home of his parents.

When the daughters marry they bring the son-in-law home to mother. The children are spoken of as belonging to the mother, and frequently remain with her in case the parents separate. Divorce is easy among the Pueblo peoples and they are strictly monogamists.

While the women do the housework and some of the lighter farm labor, the men aid in the heavier domestic duties, gather the fuel, make moccasins, weave blankets and do all the sewing, knitting and embroidering for the family.

Despite nearly four centuries of contact with white civilization, the habits of the Pueblo Indians have not materially changed. When history found them, in 1540, they dwelt in houses like their own today, tilled their farms by irrigation then as now, made baskets and produced an excellent semi-glazed pottery. They dressed in garments of cotton and buckskin and were skilled in tanning, weaving and spinning.

The Pueblo tribes are unique among the peoples of the world, enjoying two widely different religions, two sets of implements as far apart as the Stone Age and the locomotive, two sets of laws, two languages and two names.

OLLA CARRIERS RETURNING FROM WELL
ACOMA, NEW MEXICO

They Make Pottery While Their Men
Do Embroidery

Among the Pueblo peoples the making of pottery is exclusively a feminine craft. No man would make pottery—though he may decorate it—just as no woman would do embroidery, which is a man's art.

This, briefly, is the process of Pueblo pottery-making today—much the same as it has been for many centuries:

After being softened with water, a lump of clay is hollowed to form the bottom of the vessel. To this is added layer after layer of clay deftly rolled into a slender cylinder and made to adhere by pressure. The inner and outer surfaces are modeled with the hands and smoothed with a piece of gourd shell.

When the vessel has been moulded to the desired size and shape, it is placed in the sun to dry. After being smoothed with a polishing-stone, coated with a thin slip of fine clay and polished again, it is ready for painting. The painting is done by means of a sharpened stick or a brush of yucca fibre.

In firing, several vessels are placed, bottom-side up, on small stones and are covered with dry sheep manure—an ideal fuel for maintaining a uniform and continuous heat.

Each community has its distinctive shapes and decorative designs. The latter usually are geometric in form and symbolic in character; sometimes they are realistic representations of birds and animals.

A PUEBLO POTTERY MAKER

Artist-Priests Who Make Wonderful Paintings in the Sand

In the beginnings of all aboriginal art, there is a close association of painting, music, poetry, drama and the dance. In the highest form of Navaho art—the ceremonial sand-paintings of the Medicine Men—all of these elements are present, plus a religious *motif* that gives to the whole an added color and significance. For there is a purpose behind every sand-painting ceremony. These ceremonies are to cure the sick, to avert evil or to petition for unusual blessings.

The paintings are usually made by spreading a field of "fair white sand" on the floor of a Medicine Man's lodge. The drawing and coloring is done by spreading broad fields of colored sands outlined with lines of great accuracy and delicacy. Many helpers are needed on an important subject, as it must be completed before sunset and then destroyed. Dancing and the chanting of religious songs comprise a part of the ceremony.

The sacred paintings, which are symbolical rather than pictorial, have been handed down by one generation of Medicine Men to another for countless centuries. No material record is kept of the paintings or the chants, the memory of the priests being the sole medium of perpetuation.

Reproductions of several sand-paintings may be seen upon the lobby walls of *El Navajo*, the Santa Fe Hotel, at Gallup, New Mexico. The authenticity of these reproductions has been firmly established, since upon the opening of the Hotel they were dedicated with the Navahos' "Blessing-of-the-House" ceremony under the direction of the tribe's most eminent Medicine Men.

The sand-painting shown in the illustration is that of "The Grinding Snakes." It is made on the last day of a nine-days' ceremony and is used only on rare and important occasions.

NAVAHOS MAKING A SAND-PAINTING

A Commercial Expedition in Navaho Land

The commercial instinct is by no means lacking among the Navaho. In fact "swapping" has always been a popular pastime with most of the tribes, the commodities exchanged ranging from beads to ponies and wives.

The blankets and silver work of the Navaho were always sought by the other tribes. In other days the Shoshones came from what is now Wyoming and Idaho to trade beautifully tanned buckskin garments for Navaho blankets and silver trinkets. Nowadays the Navaho set off in little groups on horseback, bringing their wares to the white traders.

They are shrewd and businesslike, widely different from the popular idea of some other Indians who will exchange their earthly possessions for a plug of tobacco and a handful of beads.

There are many smiths among the Navaho, who forge iron, brass and silver. It is generally believed they learned this art from the Spaniards. At the time of the Spanish conquest, however, the Mexican tribes had a considerable knowledge of metal work and it is possible that the Navaho acquired it from them.

NAVAHO HORSEMEN

A People Made Famous by the Art of Weaving

When the European first discovered the American Indians of the Southwest, he found them weaving blankets and other garments of their own design, made chiefly of cotton which they grew, cleaned, carded, spun and dyed themselves. These blankets were not made of wool, for, prior to the coming of the Spaniards, wool was unknown in North America.

It is generally assumed that the art of weaving on the loom was learned by the Navahos from their Pueblo neighbors. At any rate, it is freely conceded that they are by far the better weavers today. In quality of work and excellence of design, all other tribes must yield to the Navaho whose art is also freest from European influence.

In speaking of the Navaho as a weaver, it should be borne in mind that it is his womankind who do the actual work. The Navaho man is seldom a weaver. Now and again one is found who is accomplished in the art, but this is a rare occurrence. It is the Navaho woman who chooses the poles and sticks for the loom, who superintends the daily life of the sheep that provide the wool, who shears the sheep, washes, cards, and spins the wool, who prepares the dyes—whether the almost-forgotten native dyes or the easily made anilines—who conceives the design, prepares the warp, actually weaves the blanket, and generally disposes of it to the trader.

In the illustration the vertical threads are the warp threads; the weft is inserted between them. The rods across the center of the blanket are inserted among the threads of the warp to separate them and to facilitate the insertion of the weft thread. In principle the loom used today by the Navaho closely resembles that of the ancient Egyptians.

A NAVAHO WEAVER

An Exposition of Indian Arts and Crafts

"They are artists primitive and ancient as regards their source, but are at the same time modern as any of the modernists in their art. One only has to note that the modern interior decorators of Europe are using Navaho rugs and Pueblo pottery for their modern interiors to verify this. After all, so-called modern art in many applications has done nothing more than to go back to primitive art for its ideas."

So speaks the director of one of America's greatest art museums. And he continues:

"Of all American art developments today, the art centers of Europe become interested mainly in the art works of our Indians and particularly our Southwest Indians. Some day we in the United States will become equally interested, but so far it is too close to us. We travel afar for art, passing in mid-ocean, as it were, artists, archaeologists and collectors who are coming to admire and collect the art of our own Indian artists—our first American artists."

The Indian Building at Albuquerque is a veritable exposition of the craftsmanship of these "first American artists." For here are exhibited many notable collections of blankets, baskets, pottery and other Indian handicraft.

An interesting feature of The Indian Building is the workroom where native craftsmen may be seen making articles similar to those shown in the exhibits.

Many of the exhibits suggest practical uses for the various articles as furnishings and decorations.

INDIAN HANDICRAFT ADAPTED TO INTERIOR DECORATION
THE INDIAN BUILDING, ALBUQUERQUE, NEW MEXICO

An American Craft Before the White Man Came

Until some Pueblo women found their way into the tribe and brought with them the art of weaving, the Navaho dressed in skins and mats made of coarse bark or fibre. Today the name Navaho is inseparably linked with the blankets that have come to be prized as among the most striking and beautiful examples of native crafts in the new world.

In the Indian Building at Albuquerque is the finest collection of Navaho blankets in existence. Among them are a number of beautiful bayettas superior in softness of coloring and quaintness of design to the antique rugs of the Orient. A few distinctive types of this collection are shown here.

The old Hopi pattern is one of the famed bayettas, taking its name from the bayetta cloth originally made in Barcelona and brought to America by the Spaniards. Later English manufacturers produced it for the Indian trade. The Indians would barter for the cloth, unravel it and weave it in.

The old Navaho bayetta is another specimen meriting the name antique. In the middle is a slit permitting the wearer's head to come through. This form is known as the *poncho*. It is woven entirely of bayetta.

Another bayetta specimen is the chief's blanket. It is very old and has softened into an exquisite rose color.

The Acoma wedding dress was worn by the Pueblo and in several respects differs from the work of the Navaho. Instead of the border pattern being woven, it is worked out in relief with vegetable dyed wools and bayetta. The designs are emblematic of clouds and rain. The background is woven of carefully selected black wool.

Two of the best types of modern Navaho blankets are shown in the specimens in which gray predominates. The Indians obtain the gray effect simply by mixing black and white.

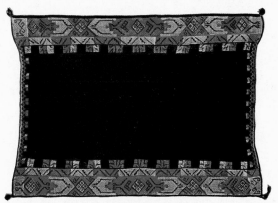

ACOMA WEDDING DRESS

MODERN

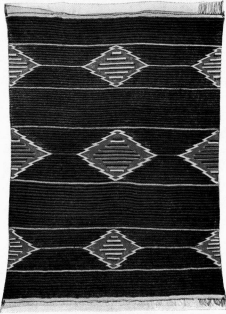

OLD HOPI PATTERN

OLD NAVAHO-BAYETTA

OLD BAYETTA CHIEFS BLANKET

MODERN

INDIAN BLANKETS

Indian Farmers Who Are Good
Hunters, Too

When the Spanish explorers wandered up from Mexico in 1540 they found, on the two banks of the Taos river, the pueblo of Taos. The Taos Indians still live in their old town, making their living from agriculture and hunting. The name *Pueblo* comes, of course, from the Spanish word meaning village and as applied to the Indians refers to the numerous small tribes that live in towns.

In early times the Pueblo peoples domesticated the wild turkey and herded them in large flocks as they now herd goats and sheep. Eagles were trapped and kept captive to supply feathers for their ceremonial dress—a practice still followed by these tribes.

The antelope, bear, deer and mountain lion also fell before the arrow of the Pueblo, and regular expeditions were made to the buffalo herds on the plains. They still have rabbit drives, the men and boys encircling a large area and gradually closing in. The little animals are then killed with boomerangs or with arrows and sticks.

Fish they never eat; it is a part of their belief that the souls of the bad women after death pass into fish. Many Pueblo clans are also forbidden the use of certain animals as food, and these laws are scrupulously observed.

THE HUNT—TAOS INDIAN

A Pair of Picturesque Farm Owners From the Ancient Town of Taos

When Hernando de Alvarado, an officer in Coronado's army, was touring New Mexico, he came upon the pueblo of Taos. Here is a description of it taken from one of the narratives of the expedition: "The houses are very close together and have five or six stories, three of them with mud walls and two or three with thin wooden walls. It is the most populous village of all the country; we estimated there were 15,000 persons in it."

That was in 1540, almost four centuries ago, and while Coronado's historians doubtless greatly overestimated the population, there is no question that Taos was a large and prosperous pueblo in those days. Today it has a population of about half a thousand. The reduction in numbers was largely due to the centuries of warfare with the whites as well as with northern Indians.

The pueblo is located fifty-eight miles northeast of Santa Fe, New Mexico. Unlike the other Pueblo Indians, the men wear their hair in two long plaits, hanging at the sides. They are active agriculturists, own good lands and live in little one-room houses on their farms in summer. After harvest they return to the pueblo. The old houses of the Spanish days are still in use, and around a portion of the village may be seen remnants of the ancient defensive wall.

TAOS INDIANS ON SCOUTING EXPEDITION

The Little Indians Have Their Emotions

In its joys and momentary griefs the Indian child does not differ much from its pale face cousin back East or over the water. This little Pueblo girl is broken hearted over the loss of a striped stick of candy which, needless to say, was replaced before the squall fairly began. A bit of candy is a rare luxury for the Indian children and they love it almost above everything.

The responsibilities of the girl children begin early; they become nursemaids to younger brothers and sisters before the white child has learned to dress. Meanwhile the boys are at play— Indian boys have rather an easy time of it.

In their strict obedience and reverence for their parents the little Indians set a good example to other children. In turn their parents are very kind, rarely inflicting punishment and seldom whipping them except in certain ceremonials when the boys are initiated into the Katcina orders during the great Powamu ceremony.

AN ARIZONA SQUALL

The Hopi's Theory of the Origin of Man

Until the Spaniards came the Hopi Indians had no conception of one Great Spirit, although they have always been pre-eminently a religious people. They deified the nature powers, the Sky God and the Mother Earth—the one the Father and the other the Mother of the races of men. In their mythology the human race was not created, but was generated by the Grand Canyon.

While other Pueblo tribes have to some extent accepted the teachings of the missionaries, the Hopi still adhere to their primitive beliefs and rites.

Their religious ceremonies, in which rain and growth of crops are the underlying *motif*, are usually held in a kiva, or underground chamber. Women are not permitted to enter the kiva except to bring food to the celebrants. Some of these ceremonials last nine days. Many of their religious songs possess real musical merit.

A SONG IN THE KIVA

Their Picturesque Beauty Attracts
the Artist

Primitive peoples unconsciously group themselves with an effect pleasing to the eye of the artist—"they make the picture" to a degree that deliberate posing can seldom attain.

There is an example of this in the picture of the Hopi mother and two children, painted from a photographic study. The little figure with leg gracefully poised, a mystical smile illuminating his face, might well be a "Saint John" by one of the old masters and "A Hopi Saint John" could properly be the title for the illustration. Even so, these little Hopi are hardly unusual specimens, for both boys and girls have exceptionally good features.

Mishongnovi, the pueblo where this picture was made, is in northeastern Arizona, its name signifying "at the place of the other which remains erect." It refers to two stone pillars, one of which has fallen, the sole remains of the old pueblo abandoned in 1680. The village that took its place now has a population of about two hundred.

A HOPI FAMILY

With Flutes They Pray to the Rain Gods

Of great importance among the Hopi is the Flute Society which controls the Annual Flute ceremony. The eternal cry for water underlies this ritual, and their every prayer is to the Gods of the Rain Clouds.

The ceremony begins in August, when the springs are drying, and a room in the house of one of the leading members of the Society is used as a ceremonial chamber. Before an altar bearing symbols of rain clouds and lightning, the men sing sacred traditional songs. The priests proceed to a distant spring where elaborate ceremonies take place around two altars and at the spring during the day.

On the afternoon of the ninth day, a great foot race is held. The men, stripped to the skin, start from a point far in the desert and run at their topmost speed towards the village. The winners are rewarded with consecrated ceremonial objects and these are buried in the owner's field, to insure the success of his crops.

Meanwhile the priests lead a slow procession to a certain spring near the village, where there are more songs and impressive rituals, accompanied by the droning of flutes. The ceremony at an end, all proceed slowly to the village, observing many sacred rites as they enter. The ceremonies terminate in the ancestral home of the Flute Society.

HOPI FLUTE BOY

Taking the Elevator in Hopiland

To enter a Hopi house one takes a ladder which leads to the roof of the first story; then another ladder to the second story or terrace, and still another to the third. The first story is used as a store room and the roof as a yard where the family may bask and sun themselves in security.

This style of architecture was a necessity in the days of tribal warfare. Perched on the summit of almost inaccessible mesas, the Hopi houses were impregnable so long as the supplies in the first story held out. In this storeroom corn was stacked as neatly as cord wood; great earthen-ware vessels contained the water supply; pumpkins, dried peaches and watermelons were heaped up for the winter, for the Hopi have always been good farmers and fruit growers.

The second floor of a Hopi house is usually the living room, with a floor of hard clay, neat and clean; the walls are tinted. Niches in the walls contain vessels of clay for cooking purposes; from pegs in the walls and ceiling are suspended clothes, children's playthings and similar objects of the household.

The Hopi women are the house builders, and at the same time the house owners. Husband has the privilege of the household, just so long as he is on his good behavior, and wife is the sole judge. One lapse and he finds his clothes, tied in a neat bundle, just outside the door.

TAKING THE ELEVATOR, HOPILAND

In a Hopi Beauty Parlor

When the little Hopi girl becomes of marriageable age a change in coiffure announces it to the pueblo's society. The proud mother takes her daughter in hand and arranges her hair in great whorls at the sides of her head, in imitation of the squash blossoms. In Hopiland the squash flower is the symbol of purity. On marriage the squash blossom head dress is abandoned; the hair of the women is then parted in the middle and hangs in two strands over the shoulders in front.

The young people of Hopiland have good features— straight noses, high cheek bones, and a skin in which the reddish hue is quite marked. The hair is usually straight and black, but in some few instances it is wavy and brown.

Industry is a tribal trait and the Hopi show great skill in weaving and dyeing. They are, in fact, the tailors for Indians of other tribes, taking food in exchange for clothing. The black blanket worn by the Hopi women is an important article of commerce among other southwestern Indians. The Hopi are extensive basket weavers, their sacred meal plaques being, perhaps, the best example of their proficiency in this art. Pottery is made in one of the villages.

In their dramatic exhibitions they surpass all other Indians of North America. Masks in great variety of decoration are made from hides, dolls are carved and dressed, mechanical toys devised to represent birds and animals and all are used in their entertainments and ceremonies.

HOPI MOTHER AND DAUGHTER

Homesites Miles From Wood and Water

In other days the Hopi built their homes on the tops of the most inaccessible mesas. It meant defense and protection for them, but it also meant hardship, for they were far from wood and water. To this day they live in these fastnesses and the women toil up the steep mesas, carrying water from the springs far down in the valley. The men go miles for wood and frequently keep their herds at some distance from their mountain homes.

The squaw shown in the illustration is of the Tewa village in northeastern Arizona. She wears a blanket and when she affects moccasins the soles are made of ox-hide, with leggings of buckskin. Ear pendants are often made of small, thin wooden blocks, ornamented with turquoise mosaic.

Hopi girls are married at the ages of fifteen and sixteen and as they grow older they age rapidly and tend to corpulency. Bachelors and spinsters are rare.

The Hopi are a peaceful people—their very name signifies "peace." Theft is rare and murder unknown; in fact crime is so unusual they seem to have no punishments except for sorcery.

CARRYING WATER TO TEWA

The Indian Who Understands Rattlesnakes

That a people should have for centuries engaged in a ceremony known as the snake dance, in which the celebrants not only handle poisonous serpents, but even take them between their teeth, naturally suggests a state of barbarism close to the lowest degradation. And yet the Hopi, the Indians of the snake dance, have been among the most peaceful of the American tribes, thrifty and industrious and of unusually high moral standards.

The snake dance is held every year in some of the villages and it is in fact a prayer for rain. Four days are spent in hunting snakes. As a coiled rattlesnake is spied, a pinch of sacred meal is cast upon the serpent, and a prayer addressed to it. Then the Indian waves the snake whip—a stick with two long buzzard feathers at the end—slowly over the reptile and as it coils he seizes it and slips it into a buckskin sack.

The reptiles are taken to the kiva and there transferred to the snake jars. On the ninth day they are bathed in a basin of sacred water. The snakes glide about seeking escape, but the men and little boys herd them back with their whips.

At sun-down the snakes are carried to the plaza, where there is singing and dancing. As one priest takes a snake in his mouth, the other attracts its attention with the whip of feathers. When the dance is over the snakes are carried to the foot of the mesa and set free.

How is it that the priests—some of them boys—are not bitten? There seems to be only one answer—the Hopi snake priests understand rattlesnakes. Perhaps the reckless confidence of the Indian makes the snake think more of flight than fight. One thing is certain, the Indians do not draw the fangs or do anything else to make the snakes harmless. Yet few Hopi priests have been known to suffer from the bite of a rattlesnake.

HOPI SNAKE DANCE

A Hopi Dwelling of Other Centuries Reproduced

Almost at the edge of the Grand Canyon and adjoining El Tovar Hotel stands an exact reproduction of a typical Hopi dwelling of a hundred years ago. It is three stories high and is of rough stone, just as the Hopi of other generations built the community houses that were forts as well.

While this is distinctively a Hopi house in design and construction, it is primarily a museum of the Indian arts and crafts, and selected representatives of several tribes demonstrate their work there. The potters, the blanket weavers and the basket makers, men and women, may be seen here, pursuing the arts as did their ancestors centuries before them.

Several rooms of the Hopi House are given over to collections of blankets, pottery and basketry that have been on exhibition in the International Expositions. The result of years of search among the people of mountain, plain and desert, they are known and valued by students of early America the world over.

THE HOPI HOUSE
GRAND CANYON NATIONAL PARK, ARIZONA

Replica of a Kiva, Where the Hopi Hold Sacred Ceremonials

Secret societies have been in existence among the Hopi for centuries and their rites are performed in underground rooms, or kivas. An exact reproduction of the interior of one of these ceremonial chambers is maintained in the Hopi House at Grand Canyon.

The altar shown here is that of the Powamu Society. The God of Germination is represented by the largest of the three idols; the next is the God of Thunder and the small black figure is Pookong, the God of War.

The banquette, or wall seat, about three sides of the room, is used by the assisting priests. The floor is of rough flat stones, loosely fitted together, the interstices occupied by smaller stones. On the walls are symbolic drawings.

What appears to be a rug in the foreground is in reality a sand-painting or mosaic. The mosaics of no two ceremonies are alike. In preparing them the priest first sprinkles brown sand on the floor. Over this various colors of sand are laid, trickling through the thumb and forefinger. Usually the squash blossom, emblem of fertility and purity, and rain clouds in black appear in the decorations. The Hopi are an agricultural people living in a dry land and in their symbols and ceremonies reference to rain is usually present.

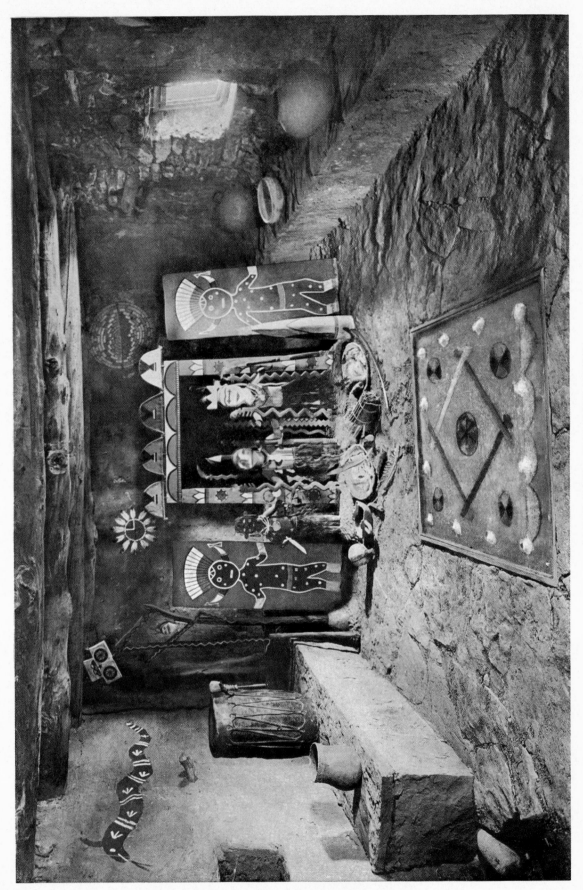

ALTAR ROOM, THE HOPI HOUSE
GRAND CANYON NATIONAL PARK, ARIZONA

Mysterious Towers Built A Thousand Years Ago

On every continent of the globe there are ruins of ancient tower-like structures, the origins and purposes of which long have been puzzles to the archaeologist.

Some of these ruins are found in our own Southwest, the remnants of towers built—so the scientists say—by the prehistoric ancestors of the Pueblo peoples.

Many theories have been advanced concerning the purposes for which these Indian towers were built, many centuries before the coming of the white man. The fact that some of the buildings undoubtedly were of considerable height and were located at points of vantage—on the sides of high cliffs or on the rims of canyons—has led certain scientists to conclude that they were ceremonial towers, astronomical observatories or military lookouts. Possibly they were used for all of these purposes.

A re-creation of these ancient Indian towers now stands on the brink of the Grand Canyon of the Colorado River. Upon a high, rocky promontory on the South Rim, this watchtower rises from a huge foundation of Canyon boulders. At its base is a low, round *kiva*, a reproduction of the prehistoric ceremonial chambers of the Pueblo Indians.

The tower is constructed of native rocks and blends naturally into the walls of the Canyon, appearing to have stood there through long ages. Nearby is the reproduction of a typical ruin, showing the condition in which the remnants of prehistoric Indian buildings usually are found. Today there are many such ruins along the rim of the Grand Canyon.

Embedded in the inner walls of the watchtower there are a number of Indian pictographs, transferred from the rock-surfaces of caves and cliffs where they were carved by aboriginal artists in prehistoric times. The walls also contain many faithful reproductions of these strange picture-writings, as well as groups of symbolic paintings by a modern Hopi artist.

From its great height, The Indian Watchtower commands a sweeping panorama of the Painted Desert, Tusayan Forest and distant mountain-peaks—and breath-taking views of the mightiest of all spectacles, the Grand Canyon.

THE INDIAN WATCHTOWER
GRAND CANYON NATIONAL PARK, ARIZONA

Where Woman is the Perpetuator
of the Arts

The Indian woman was not only the originator of the arts among the native Americans, but she has been their zealous perpetuator as well. Let it be basketry, pottery or, in some tribes, weaving, the skill is with the woman.

Far over in northeastern Arizona is a little Hopi village of fewer than two hundred inhabitants, seldom visited by the whites. It would be little known except for one household, whose fame is due wholly to Nampeyo—Nampeyo of the village of Tewa.

Every student of Indian ceramics knows of Nampeyo, for she is foremost among the Indians of today in the perpetuation of this art. It is probably safe to say that the beautiful polychrome vases of this woman and her family are the most artistic among Indian products.

In making pottery the Indian uses neither measure, model nor potter's wheel. All is done from memory and with the hands. A few tools, hardly more than sticks and brushes made from yucca leaves, are the instruments. In the uses of materials, the clays and pigments, the methods are as complex as the tools are simple. The Indians go miles for clay that will burn a certain shade and the colors, almost impervious to acids, are made of stonelike substances ground to dust in mortars and made liquid.

The decorations are often strongly symbolic, for there are few peoples possessing the sense of the mystic more than the Hopi. In form the articles of pottery range from spoons or ladles to cups, water vessels and elaborately decorated vases.

HOPI WOMAN DECORATING POTTERY

Never Were Two Pieces of Indian Pottery Exactly Alike

The culture center of the early Americans was in the Pueblo region of the Southwest. These people as aborigines expressed their art sense in the making of pottery.

Today the Pueblo tribes of New Mexico and Arizona practice the art in its aboriginal form with little or no variation. For tempering purposes the clay was mixed with sand, pulverized stone and shells. The art was restricted almost exclusively to the women, a condition that holds good today. The potter's wheel was unknown to these people before the white men came, and even now its use is rare.

The colors usually employed are black, white, yellow, red and brown. Geometric and symbolic designs are the most popular, with the triangle predominating; many of them indicate lightning, rain and clouds. Next in frequency are the figures derived from birds and animals, and last come the decorations suggested by leaves and flowers. The sunflower appears often in the floral designs.

The Indian potters work neither by rule nor pattern, so that while only a few general forms are used, no two of the vessels are the same size or form. The same holds good of the ornamentation. The vessels vary in size from the large vase, holding ten gallons or more, to the little cup or canteen of a half pint or less.

Some of the work, such as the black Santa Clara specimen, is lustrous and at first glance would appear to be glazed. That is not the case, however, for the Indians never fully mastered the use of salt in the clay mixtures. The sheen on the Santa Clara specimen comes from careful rubbing with a polishing stone.

SANTO DOMINGO

HOPI

ACOMA

HOPI

SANTA CLARA

MARICOPA

VERY OLD ZUNI

PREHISTORIC HOPI

PREHISTORIC PUEBLO LAMP

PREHISTORIC WATER JAR FROM CLIFF DWELLER RUINS

PREHISTORIC

INDIAN POTTERY

The Pima, Who Call Themselves "The People"

The name *Pima* means "no" and the tribe received its negative appellation through a misunderstanding of the missionaries. These Indians themselves confidently use a tribal name signifying "The People." They are probably of Aztec origin and centuries ago they built houses of adobe, strong and substantial, but some of their Eastern neighbors, notably the ever-warlike Apaches, raided their well-established villages and drove them to dome-shaped lodges of pliable poles, covered with thatch and mud. And in these they have lived ever since under conditions almost identical with those of four centuries ago.

The hooting of an owl brings fear to a Pima. He believes that it is a sign of death—that the owl is the messenger carrying the soul from the dying to another world.

They never consider marriage binding, husband and wife separating at will and marrying again at will. The women do all the heavy work, except hunting, plowing and sewing; when the family moves the husband usually rides and the wife walks, carrying a papoose or even a part of the grain she herself has harvested.

The grain is threshed by the stamping of horses and winnowed by the women, who skillfully toss it from flat baskets. Wheat is now their staple crop and in good years they sell some to the whites. On reaching market the husband sometimes has no compunctions about trading the crop and handiwork of the women for articles for his own personal adornment.

A DESERT NURSERY
PIMA MOTHER AND CHILD

The Pima Women, Who Make Baskets

In basketry the Indian woman has left the best witness of what she could do in handiwork and expression. Originally the baskets were wholly without decoration, and so crude as not to entitle them to consideration. The larger baskets were used to carry corn, melons and peppers and the smaller ones were used for holding beans, shelled corn and other coarse materials.

The decorative element appeared in the work centuries ago, the ancient ruins giving up specimens of delicate weave embellished with geometric and symbolic designs. Figures of human beings, animals and leaves were woven in and today the same designs are followed in the better work.

The Pima and Apache originally used geometric figures in their designs, but of later years the Apache in particular have combined these with human and animal figures. In weave, material and coloring the work of the Pima and of the White Mountain Apache is almost identical.

In making baskets the Pima woman uses the fibre of the yucca. Wrapping this fibre with the same material, she forms a fine rope, or thread. The weaving begins at the center or bottom of the plaque, bowl or jug that is to be evolved. The body is usually yellow, highly ornamented in black or white.

The Pima, now living in the valleys of the Gila and Salt Rivers in Arizona, came from northeastern Mexico. The ruins of large irrigation and defensive works built by them centuries ago still are to be seen.

PIMA INDIAN BASKET MAKER

An Apache Grand Dame Weaving
a Supply Basket

It is stretching the imagination to connect this peaceful scene of household industry with the word *Apache*, for that name has come to mean everything cruel and bloodthirsty to the last degree. But where one or two groups honestly and conscientiously earned their reputation for murderous cunning, the tribe as a whole has been greatly maligned.

The old mother peacefully, contentedly weaving herself into a basket is an Apache, every drop of her blood, as much as Victorio or Geronimo when they were murdering settlers and baffling the United States government.

Yet, with all the evidence of her domesticity, this Apache matron is by no means a paragon. For one thing, she is a gambler to the marrow; gambling is a national pastime among the Apache men and women. They have games with sticks that are thrown into a circle, counting according to whether the round or flat side falls upward. They use Spanish cards, and full decks made of horsehide and marked with great care are not unusual.

All of the Apache women make baskets. Some of them are water-tight and are used as jugs. The one grandmother is weaving about herself is a storage basket for grains and vegetables.

WEAVING AN APACHE GRANARY

Basketry Still is a Living Art Among
Certain of the Indians

While relatively few of the American Indian tribes understood the making of pottery, except in the crudest form, it may be said that every Indian—from the land of the Eskimo down through Mexico—was a basket weaver. True, to many it meant little more than the plaiting of coarse willows for a cradle, a grain receptacle or even to be used as shelter and clothing.

Contrast this purely utilitarian basketry with the delicate weave of the Pomo Indians—500 stitches to the square inch. Then there is the work of the Tulare people, who weave yarn in with the vegetable fibre. The wedding plaque used in the Navaho marriage ceremony is an interesting piece of basketry, but, strangely enough, is made by the Paiute Indians. Other tribes known chiefly for their fibre-weaving are the Inyo, the Chimehuevi, the Mission and the Hupa.

The Apaches, usually thought of as warriors, are experts in basket making and each of the three great divisions of this tribe—Jicarilla, Mescalero and White Mountain—shows distinctive characteristics in the art. Some of the Apaches weave the fibre braids so closely that the basket becomes water-tight without further preparation. Ordinarily the baskets are made water-tight by the application of *pinon* pitch inside and out.

PIMA TRAY

PITCHED WATER BOTTLE

ORAIBI (HOPI)

APACHE BURDEN

APACHE STORAGE

HUPA SQUAW CAP

HOPI KATCINA
TRAY

TULARE

PAIUTE
WEDDING BASKET

INDIAN BASKETS

The Problem of Existence as Met by a Desert People

Were all the rest of America laid waste, the people of Hopiland could go on living with very little change in their daily routine. They can grow everything they eat and can make everything they wear.

When one considers the obstacles overcome day after day by these Indians of the desert the feeling towards them can be nothing less than admiration. They had to build their homes on mountain tops for protection against marauders. Their fields, at times miles away and poor enough in themselves, gave forth very scanty crops unless water was led to them. The quest for fuel meant a journey far from the little fortress of a home on the mesa.

The illustration shows one of these fuel trains homeward bound. The burros are laden with bits of cedar and *pinon*, gathered miles away. Notice the sturdy, businesslike stride of the man in white—it is one not popularly associated with the Indian. In the distance, on the very top of the mountain, the angular outlines of the village appear. Soon the sure-footed little burros will be clambering up the steep path and the women and children will stack the wood away to be used in the ovens and in the fireplaces on cold days. Gathering wood is one of the main occupations of the Hopi between the time of planting and harvesting.

INDIAN WOOD TRAIN ON THE ARIZONA DESERT

The Supai, Who Live in the Grand Canyon

In the great kaleidoscopic chasm feebly termed "The Grand Canyon," in a setting of ever changing blues and golds and purples, live the Havasupai, a small tribe of Yuman stock and commonly known as the Supai. Their homes are of twigs and poles covered with earth. In the days of buckskin their leather work possessed considerable merit, but it was lost with the introduction of clothing from the white man's mills.

They are sufficiently versed in agriculture to grow corn, melons and products on which they subsist in summer. In the winter, game from the surrounding mountains keeps them in food. There are about 150 of the Supai left in their highly colored little valley and they have been steadily declining in numbers.

Basket making is the art of the women of the Supai. In other days the Supai were extravagantly addicted to the use of cosmetics. Both men and women covered their faces with smooth coatings of red ocher or a blue paint made from the wild indigo plant. These decorations were not the war paint customary among other tribes, but were worn as an everyday ornament.

They knew little about pottery, but met the situation by making baskets, coating them with clay and using them as cooking utensils. All basket-making Indians know the time and season for digging the plants, how to dry, prepare and preserve the tough and pliable parts for use and to reject the brittle. They have knowledge of dyes, and for tools they use their nimble fingers and sharp stones, a bone awl and a shell for polishing. In these days, scissors, knives and steel awls have been added. The largest basket made by them is for burden purposes and the squaws often use them as papoose carriers. Another is in the shape of a bowl and a third is a bottle, made water-proof by means of *pinon* pitch.

A SUPAI CORNFIELD
CATARACT CANYON, ARIZONA

The Story of the Thunder-Bird

(Illustrated on Title Page)

In the mythology of all the Indians of North America birds play a most prominent part, and of them all the Thunder-Bird is the most frequently encountered. Growing out of the effort of primitive man to account for the natural phenomena surrounding him, the myth of the Thunder-Bird varies as to detail with almost every tribe, but with most of them it is held responsible for the lightning and thunder; and with some for the rain. The species varies with the different tribes. With some it is shaped as an eagle, with others as a hawk, with others as a grouse, and with still others as a mighty monster of unknown form.

The wide extent of this myth is evidenced by the fact that the Thunder-Bird figures prominently in the mythology of the Eskimo, the Northwest Indians, the Navaho, the Plains Indians and the Pueblo peoples.

The Plains tribes believe the thunderstorm is due to a conflict between the Thunder-Bird and a giant rattlesnake. Among other tribes the Thunder-Bird is pictured as dwelling in the mountains with kindred spirits and sallying forth at intervals to cause the lightning by the opening and closing of its eyes, the thunder by the beating of its all-enveloping wings, while the rain falls from a lake carried on its back.

With the primitive people of the arid Southwest water is the most precious of all elements. The Southwestern Indian depends chiefly upon his crops and his flocks and herds for livelihood. Particularly is this true of the Pueblo peoples. To these Indians the coming of the Thunder-Bird means rich grass for their flocks and herds, abundant crops, full granaries, and so the Bird is a deity embodying all things beneficent and kind; its presence a constant augury of peace and happiness; its painted image on the rocks and in the *estufas* an enduring talisman of good fortune.

On the cliffs over-shadowing the ancient ruins of one of the New Mexico pueblos is a picture of the Thunder-Bird. It is about ten feet square, in black and white on red sandstone. The mineral paints used by the prehistoric artists have remained bright and clear and today that figure on the red cliff is generally accepted as the authentic design of this universal Indian deity.

A SUPAI INDIAN

W. P. GOSHORN PRINTING CO.
KANSAS CITY, MO.